# Paul Gauguin

## A Journey to Tahiti

Parau Api

P Gauguin 92

Prestel

The painter Paul Gauguin is going off on a long journey to the South Seas. He has sailed to distant countries several times before, but this journey is to be his longest and most exciting, he is sure of that. He packs his suitcase and a number of boxes and says goodbye to his wife and children. "Isn't it going to be dangerous living somewhere so far away?" his daughter Aline asks. "I don't know," he replies, "but I will take good care of myself and write to you— and I will definitely be coming back."

He takes the train from Paris to Marseilles where the big port is full of steamships. Gauguin's journey by ship takes almost two months and for much of the time there is nothing to see except water and sky.

2

Fatata te Miti

One morning an island appears on the horizon. To start with it is just a little dot, but as the ship draws closer, Gauguin can make out the steep mountains covered with trees and can see a white beach.

# Tahiti!

It is almost dark again by the time the ship drops anchor in the little port of Papeete, the capital of the island.

Tahiti is one of several thousand little islands dotted around the South Seas. The colors and the smell of the plants, the houses, the skies and the people—everything is very different here to back home in Paris.

The steamship 'The Cross of the South' in the port of Papeete. Photograph: Charles Spitz

The Tahitians come up to the painter,
staring and giggling, as Gauguin is much
taller and has long hair. Only the women
on Tahiti have long hair, not the men. They
call Gauguin 'Taata-vahine,' which means
'man-woman', although he can't
understand their language yet.

4

There are also other Europeans on the island—who, like Gauguin, are French. Most of the men wear uniform and the women white dresses. Tahiti is a French colony, which means that it 'belongs' to France and French troops live on the island. Although the native Tahitians have their own government and even their own king, they have no direct part in the politics or administration of their island. Instead it is run by the white Europeans who don't seem to like being in the South Seas very much. They are not used to such a hot climate and are often ill as a result. They keep their distance from the native islanders as they don't speak their language and do not understand their culture. It all seems very strange to them.

The Governor of the island and his colonial officers. Papeete, c. 1893

Gauguin's house on Tahiti.
Photograph: Charles Spitz, 1892

Te raau rahi

Paul Gauguin is different from the other Europeans. He tries to make friends with the native islanders. He moves into a simple house on the outskirts of the small town of Papeete where there are hardly any other French people. The Tahitians are very curious and start coming to Gauguin's house. What could be in the big boxes that he has, they wonder.

One after another, Gauguin unpacks his boxes and brings out an easel, lots and lots of tubes of paint, and a number of canvases so that he can start painting pictures. The uniformed French officials and their wives think, of course, that he has come to paint them. But Gauguin has little interest in his fellow Europeans. He prefers to paint the dark-skinned faces of the Tahitian women who come and visit him. Their clothes are patterned with stripes, dots and flowers in dazzling colors. After just a short time, Gauguin has to ask for more tubes of yellow, orange, and pink paint to be sent from France as he uses up so much of these colors in his paintings.

This is a picture that Gauguin never finished and it makes it easier for us to see how he worked. First of all he made a pencil drawing and then went over these sketches in a dark-blue color. Oil paint was added at the next stage. He used blues and browns instead of black for the dark colored areas.

After a few days, Gauguin gets to know a young girl called Tehamana who can speak a little French. She laughs when Gauguin asks if he can paint her portrait and then tries to find out why a French artist should want to come to her island. Gauguin tells her about the lively but tiring life in the big city of Paris. While living there he felt that there must be more to life than streets of expensive shops, elegantly dressed ladies and people spoilt by luxury and decided that Paris was not the place for him.

He longed to lead a simple life with ordinary people in exotic, natural surroundings. That is why he came to Tahiti even though his friends said that he must be mad (but perhaps, really, they are a bit jealous).

After Gauguin has been living in the small town of Papeete for a little while, he decides to move on. Tahiti is not quite as he had expected. The white Europeans have kept their own culture and religion which they believe to be so much better and have not tried to understand the Tahitian way of life.

Gauguin sets out to find a better place. He wants to be with the native islanders who live in villages deep in the countryside. He wants to find out how they live, what they eat and drink and, most of all, what they believe in. Tehamana leads him through the forest to a river. Gauguin takes his paints and canvases with him and rents a little hut made of bamboo with a roof of palm leaves. The few dishes that he takes with him are broken accidentally on the journey, so he carves a bowl from a piece of wood and decorates it with an unusual pattern. He buys a spear and tries to catch fish, just like the local people do. He has also brought a rifle with him, but hunting is difficult in the thick forest around the village.

He eats a lot of boiled wild bananas (which taste more like a kind of vegetable) and *pol*, which is made from the local breadfruit trees. This fruit is ground and made into a type of porridge or baked in an oven dug into the earth to produce a kind of pudding. Coconuts and mangoes grow on the trees around about and now and again he eats chicken too. The little black pigs that can be seen running around everywhere are only eaten on special occasions when they are roasted over an open fire.

At night it can be a little frightening.
When it gets dark, the animals come
out of the jungle and walk around
between the huts. Big, colorful birds
make so much noise after sunset that
Gauguin cannot sleep. Are they really
the spirits of the dead, he wonders?

The natives of the island believe that
when someone dies, his or her spirit
carries on living. It can then become
one of the so-called 'ancestral spirits.'
Tehamana has many such ancestors
(members of her family who lived some
time ago) with whom she talks.
Sometimes she whispers and can
hardly be understood, as if she were
sharing a secret with them. Whenever
she talks to the bad spirits she tries
to calm them down.

The ancestors of the Tahitians  settled
on different groups of islands dotted
around the South Seas and in New
Zealand many many years ago, where
they still continue to hold onto their
beliefs.

In this painting, a woman has a young dog in her arms. This woman is the goddess Oviri. Oviri is 'in charge' of the ancestors and, as their goddess, she also looks after the Kingdom of the Dead. Perhaps that is why the two women behind her look so afraid. Take a closer look—have you noticed the little flower that Oviri has put behind her ear? The flower is a symbol of life and generations of children to come.

Paul Gauguin needs quite some time until he can understand exactly what the Tahitians believe in. In his paintings he often mixes his European ideas with the ideas and beliefs of the native islanders.

One day there is a big festival—
an *upaupa* as they local people
call it—and Gauguin is invited to
go along. By now he can
understand the local language
much better and he even dresses
like the native islanders. He
wraps a *parau* around his middle,
a wide piece of brightly colored
cloth, which when folded looks a
bit like a skirt. Above the waist
he doesn't wear anything and he
has become very tanned from
the sun so that he almost looks
like a rather tall Tahitian. The
elegant French ladies in towns
like Papeete find this quite
shocking!

The *upaupas* take place at night
so that the ancestral spirits can
join in. They always have to make
sure that the gods are in a good
mood. One of the little black pigs
is caught and roasted on a long
spit over the fire. The Tahitians
and their guests dance and sing
to the sound of drums the whole
night through until they are very
tired indeed.

79

d'elle en lui, par lui se dégageait, émanait un parfum de beauté qui enivrait mon âme, et où se mêlait comme une forte essence le sentiment de l'amitié produite entre nous par l'attraction mutuelle du simple et du composé.

Était-ce un homme qui marchait là devant moi? - Chez ces peuplades nues, comme chez les animaux, la différence entre les sexes est bien moins évidente que dans nos climats. Nous accentuons la faiblesse de la femme en lui épargnant les fatigues c'est-à-dire les occasions de développement, et nous la modelons d'après un menteur idéal de gracilité. A Tahiti, l'air de la forêt ou tous les poumons, élargit toutes les hanches, et les graviers de la p raÿons du soleil n'épargnent pa que les hommes. Elles font les

Gauguin keeps a diary of his time on Tahiti and draws lots of pictures to illustrate his tales. He gives this book the name *Noa Noa* which means as much as 'scented' or 'perfumed country.'

61

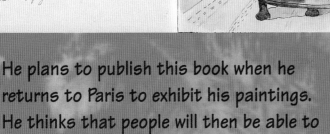

He plans to publish this book when he returns to Paris to exhibit his paintings. He thinks that people will then be able to understand his pictures better.

Every now and then he cheats a little and adds some things to his stories and adventures that are not true, or at least that didn't really happen quite like he describes. . .

Sometimes Gauguin receives letters from home. His friends want to know how he is getting on. They think that he is living among 'uncivilized' people and are worried about him.

They needn't be worried, as Gauguin has found so many new things that he can't stop painting. Later on, however, he sails back to Europe with a lot of his paintings, which are then shown at an exhibition in Paris.

22

Some of Gauguin's friends in front of the guesthouse 'Gloanec' in Pont-Aven, in the north of France

The Parisians are very surprised when they see his paintings. Everything he paints is different to what they have ever seen before. Unfamiliar, beautiful people, exotic plants and trees, and the colors—especially the bright oranges and pinks. Of course nobody in Paris knows anything about the goddess Oviri or Tehamana's ancestors. Some find it all a bit difficult to understand— the subjects Gauguin paints are exotic and new. It is only later when the people in Europe have got to know Gauguin's art much better, that he becomes a very famous painter. In the history of modern art, Gauguin has since become just as important as the two other great artists of his time, Paul Cézanne and Vincent van Gogh.

After two years on Tahiti, Gauguin decides to return to France. He has made many new friends but he often feels lonely and homesick. He carefully packs all his paintings in the big boxes and has them loaded on a ship in the port of Papeete. When he boards the ship, Tehamana stays behind and waves him goodbye.

Gauguin takes lots of things from Tahiti with him. In Paris he even wears his brightly colored *parau* and he makes his artist's studio look like the hut he had down by the river. He hangs the spear on the wall and puts wooden figures of goddesses on colorful pieces of cloth. He has even brought a monkey with him which swings around the studio and tugs at visitors' hair! But it is winter in Paris and life is not as exciting or beautiful as in the South Seas. He wonders if his friends can begin to understand that the paradise he had found on Tahiti is actually quite different to the one he had first imagined.

He decides to carry on looking for his paradise on earth and a little later he packs his bags again to set off on yet another great journey with his easel and paints . . .

# Paul Gauguin's life

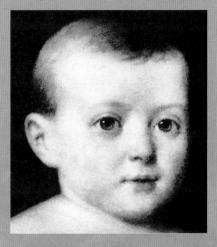

Jules Laure, Paul Gauguin Aged Two, Saint-Germain-en-Laye, Musée départmental du Prieuré

Mette Gauguin in Copenhagen, 1885

Mette and Paul Gauguin in Copenhagen, 1885

**Paul Gauguin** was born on June 7, 1848 in Paris. One year later his family emigrates to Peru where Paul, his mother and his sister, Marie-Marcelline, stay at his great uncle's (his father having died that same year). In 1855 the family returns to Paris. In 1865, aged 17, Paul joins the crew of a ship as a sailor and travels to Rio de Janeiro. One year later he sails to South America for a second time.

Gauguin's guardian, Gustave Arosa. Photograph: Nadar

In 1871 he starts to draw and paint. He meets his future wife, Mette, marries, and has five children—Emile, Aline, Clovis, Jean René, and Pola. Gauguin shows some of his paintings at an exhibition of works by Impressionist painters in 1879 and, at the same time, takes a job at an insurance company to earn some money. In 1885 he moves with his family to Copenhagen where Mette stays with the children while Gauguin returns to Paris after just a few months.

Paul Gauguin with his children Clovis and Aline in Copenhagen, 1885

Self-Portrait 'Les misérables', 1888

In 1887 Gauguin travels to Panama and works on the Panama Canal building site. He then moves to the island of Martinique where he paints twelve pictures. In 1888 and in the following year, he spends most of his time with other artists in Pont-Aven in Brittany, in the north of France, where he produces many paintings. He gets to know Vincent van Gogh and they become good friends, but following an argument they go their separate ways. Gauguin loves painting at the seaside near Le Pouldu.

One of Gauguin's letters to Vincent van Gogh, 1889

Paul Gauguin. Photograph: Harlingue-Viollet, 1893/94

Gauguin plans a long journey to the South Seas in 1890 but it is not until the spring of 1891 that he sails to Tahiti aboard the ship 'Océanie'. This is the beginning of the story told in this book!

Te arii vahine, woodcut, 1896

He arrives in Papeete on June 9 and in September moves into a small village. During this time Gauguin paints many of his most beautiful pictures.

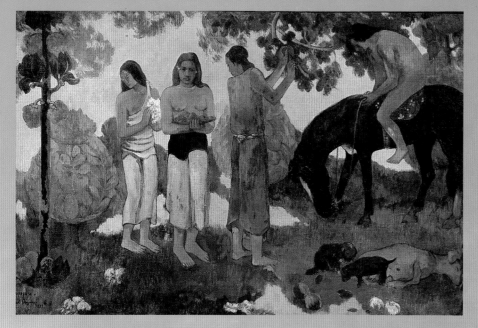

*Verdant Tahiti (Rupe rupe), 1899*

*Tahitian Girl with Fan, 1902*

In 1893 he sets out on his long journey back to France with sixty-seven paintings in his baggage. In November, the first major exhibition of his works from the South Seas is held in Paris, where he then decides to rent a studio.

In the following year he starts making new plans to move to the South Seas for the rest of his life. He arrives in Papeete again in 1895 but cannot do much painting as he is very ill. In 1901 he sells his house and the land he owned on Tahiti and takes a steamboat to the Marquesas Islands where he buys a house on the island Hiva Oa. When he refuses to pay taxes and encourages the native islanders to rise up against the colonial administration, he is taken to court.

In his absence, his book Noa Noa is published, which shows the impressions he gained during his first journey to Tahiti.

After a long illness, Paul Gauguin dies on May 9, 1903 and is buried in the little cemetery on Hiva Oa.

*Gauguin's grave in the little Catholic cemetery on Hiva Oa*